stellar nursery

stellar nursery

ON MY (TRANS) BODY
AND MY CHOICE

k.g. strayer

QUILTED PRESS

QUILTED PRESS

info@quiltedpress.com
quiltedpress.com

This book depicts actual events in the author's life as truthfully as recollection permits and/or could be verified by research. All persons within are actual individuals; there are no composite characters. Dialogue has been reconstructed from memory. The names and identifying characteristics of some individuals or the events they took part in have been changed to respect their privacy. The author in no way represents any company, corporation, or band, mentioned in this book.

Cover design: Rachel Ake
Cover images: overlays-textures/Shutterstock; Erika Anes/
Addictive Creative/Shutterstock; srifoto/Shutterstock
Interior Design: Alison Cnockaert

ISBN: 979-8-9896691-1-0 (paperback)
ISBN: 979-8-9896691-3-4 (ebook)

for Braden, Olive, and Mavis—
The family I always wanted

Find content warnings listed by page number on page 135. Please do not hesitate to visit them first if you prefer that reading experience.

I don't remember believing in God. I remember knowing that some things can be lost forever. Thinking maybe my mother was God. Loving anything the way I loved cracking open the stem of a milkweed plant was bound to end in despair. Hiding from her in the park, in the port-a-potty, practically boiling in the sun, for what seemed like hours. And I don't even remember why.

I was born without a mother. No, the tornado was my mother. I opened my mouth to drink the rain. I opened my mouth and I let something in.

As a kid, if I could have skipped eating altogether, I would have. It was safer to need less. This became embarrassing at the doctor's office, dangerously underweight. My mother told him the only things I would eat were peanut butter or happy meals. "Then peanut butter and happy meals it is," he said. Maybe that was the beginning—just keeping me alive. A certain body. A certain kind of body. Back then, happy meals came with a "girl toy" or a "boy toy." My mom would pull up to the drive-through and I would study the menu—not to make an order, I ordered the same cheeseburger happy meal with no pickles every time—but to decide which toy I wanted. "Is the happy meal for a boy or a girl?" The voice in the speaker would prompt. She would turn to me in the back seat. "What is it today? Boy or girl?"

No one escaped my mother's commentary. A constant hum of ridicule, like it kept her alive. My aunt's figure, for example, wasn't the hot little number it used to be when they were younger, when my mom was so jealous of her big boobs and all the stolen attention she received because of them. My mother remarked with glee that those same boobs made her "look so fat now." They drifted in and out of something like friendship over the years, bonding over diets, recipes to conjure food from thin air, workout routines and schedules. How bad they were for deviating.

The Milky Way contains a black hole at its core. The Sagittarius A* is the only known supermassive black hole in our galaxy. It contains the mass of about 4.3 million of our suns. A black hole's gravity is so strong that nothing can escape—not even light. This gravitational force is also responsible for the distortion of space and time in the surrounding areas. The closer you get to a black hole, the more slowly time moves.

For a long time, my aunt couldn't get pregnant. It was common knowledge in our extended family that she and my uncle wanted a child desperately, were trying for one but it kept not happening. She would be such a good mom, everyone said. They practiced with me and my brother. They would raise us if our parents died, a fact that gripped my childhood imagination. What would it have been like? Softer? Maybe. Only a little.

I survived my childhood long enough to start high school. I still wanted to leave the planet, make it all stop. Even my parents could not deny something was wrong. My limbs felt heavy, every step like pushing my way through peanut butter. My hair started falling out. I could not lift a backpack. I used to say my mother took me to the doctor because she thought I might really do it. No—looking back, it was the month I gained twelve pounds. I was barely eating, barely moving. The pediatrician told my mother I must have been hiding cheetos under my bed. It wouldn't be the first time I was called a liar.

Because the moon has no atmosphere, there are very few elements at play that could wipe away the footprints of the Apollo astronauts. But, as with everything, time will find a way to undo them. They erode, but very, very slowly. Eventually—perhaps not even in my lifetime, hundreds or thousands of years from now—the moon's surface will look untouched again.

There are right ways and wrong ways to go through puberty. At least, there are certain traditions, little stories a body is meant to tell based on its assignment. One I was failing. That's how it felt—a test. No waist, no hips, flat chest, broad shoulders. It's okay to be a tomboy, until you reach a certain age.

I felt too old to be at the pediatrician's office, anyway. My problems were too advanced. My mother found a new doctor, a specialist. He wore a bowtie, a man well into his seventies who never seemed to plan on retiring. Sometimes we would wait for upwards of two hours in his lobby. He listened to every symptom my mother described. He ran every test she asked for, and more.

Fourteen is unusually young to be diagnosed with hypothyroidism and polycystic ovarian syndrome (PCOS). My mother cried when he confirmed it. I was relieved—the tests yielded answers. I was broken, and we finally knew how. We were going to fix it. She was devastated that I would need medicine every day for the rest of my life. I was officially defective, measurably imperfect.

My mother also has hypothyroidism, the main reason she suspected mine in the first place. The PCOS diagnosis was a surprise to both of us. A *syndrome* is not quite an illness of its own, more like a collection of symptoms waiting to be swept into the same net. The doctor lifted my shirt and squinted at the hair growing beneath my belly button, down into my underwear. He called it my "happy trail." My body broken down into parts, collected back together with new instructions. Crossed out and rewritten.

Of the medicines I thought I would take every day for the rest of my life—hormonal birth control, synthroid, and spironolactone—only one was a mystery to me. I didn't know what spironolactone did, or how. I wouldn't know until I was much older. My mother told me my "body made too much testosterone," and this was why I didn't look the way I was supposed to look. I often wondered what would happen if I stopped taking it, this seemingly benign little pill, when its companions held dire consequences if I missed them. The fear on top of my fear: if I stopped, I might gain weight. So I put my questions away.

What could I have been? All kinds of too much. The first intervention.

Spironolactone has a variety of medical applications. It's used in dermatology to treat acne, and can help lower blood pressure and reduce the risk of heart failure. Its effectiveness in combating hair loss and "excess" body hair is due to its "estrogen effect." Because it acts like estrogen in the body, it may also cause breast tenderness and enlargement. It is a commonly-prescribed form of hormone-replacement therapy (HRT).

My mother taught me from a young age that breast cancer was not a risk on her side of the family, but an inevitability. My grandmother, her sisters, their mother—all died from it eventually. When I was fourteen, she had a double mastectomy, removing every trace of breast tissue from her body. She told me it was all just to be safe. She didn't have cancer *yet*, but, of course, she was smart and vigilant, especially about her body. Everything under control. And it made sense to me–that she might follow a path to break the chain of what came before.

"Boobs are just boobs," I remember her saying once, before the mastectomy. "I can't imagine risking my life to keep them."

In the case of a double mastectomy, the point is to wipe the body clean—breasts, nipples, skin, flesh, every cell extending beneath the armpits, up near the collarbone. "Reconstruction" after a double mastectomy is much the same as implants, with one critical step in-between: the remaining skin and tissue must be stretched, slowly, in order to cover the implants. How much stretching and how long it takes depends on how much skin was salvaged, how big of an implant the patient wants. Skin grafts can create textural, multi-dimensional nipples then tattooed to match their previous color. The pain of reconstruction is a consequence of feeling at home in a body that needed to change to survive.

Elaine Scarry writes: "When one hears about another person's physical pain, the events happening within that person's body may seem to have the remote character of some deep subterranean fact, belonging to an invisible geography that, however portentous, has no reality because it has not yet manifested itself on the visible surface of the earth. Or alternatively, it may seem as distant as the interstellar events referred to by scientists who speak to us mysteriously of not yet detectable intergalactic screams, or of 'very distant Seyfert galaxies, a class of objects within which violent events of unknown nature occur from time to time.'"

On a college visit to my mother's alma mater, winding our way through full tables at a cafe, she whispered conspiratorially "did you see that? All those double-takes?" She loved pointing out the way men looked at me. I kept my eyes straight ahead. I wasn't looking back. Maybe it scared her, the way I wasn't looking back.

My dad was not comfortable with the idea of breast implants. At least, that's what my mom said. I never talked to him about it myself—never would. She said he didn't love it, but she would talk to him about it for me. She would help him understand. He would understand, because this was something she'd always wanted, too. This was something she'd always wanted, too.

I saw the same doctor for my implants who performed the series of surgeries on my mother. The two of them had great rapport, like old friends. I barely spoke. I barely remember those appointments. Just that I was embarrassed. Ashamed.

At times, even I couldn't tell where she ended and I began. I was the malignant growth, removed. A part of her, broken off. Phantom cells she swore she could still feel—some critical threads never severed.

Implants can be inserted above or below the muscle. Below is more painful, a longer recovery, but a more "natural" option. "So you won't feel like a handful of silicone," the doctor said. Low, medium, and high profile described how rounded they were, how prominently they sat on my chest. Again, I picked the most realistic. I never wanted anyone to know. I just wanted a different body. To fix a mistake.

The options for how he would insert the implants came down to the kinds of scars he'd leave. The most uncomplicated way left horizontal lines beneath my chest, like two red underlines from a teacher's pen. I wasn't a good candidate for keyhole surgery, a technique that meant making the incision around the areola instead, like cutting a dress open at the seam. But we had no need to go to these lengths. Ordinary scars would do, my doctor thought. And anyway, (he winked before saying this) it wasn't like I was going to do any nude modeling in the future. My mother laughed.

Breast implant surgeries come with a disclaimer: they do not last forever. In fact, their life span is ideally around fifteen years. Beyond that, the risk for rupture increases dramatically as time goes on. The body inevitably builds scar tissue around the invader. "Fifteen years, or whenever you have a baby, whichever comes first," the doctor told me. "Who knows, maybe by then you'll want to upgrade to something bigger."

Strap the weights to my chest.

Name them shame.

Make me carry them until they kill me.

After the implant surgery, I woke up in phase one recovery. A kind man hovered over me, checking something on a monitor, unsticking medical tape. A pendant hung from a cord around his neck, a cross made of two iron nails. I felt safe. I longed for these moments, the tenderness of ether and the care of a hospital bed. I never wanted to leave. He said "this is just phase one. You won't remember me."

Every time my mother told me I needed to pluck my eyebrows, bleach the hair on my upper lip, shave my big toe—was it sleight-of-hand? Hiding in plain sight? An appearance that was mostly disappearance. Shaving, shrinking, deleting. She would stop in the middle of a conversation, distracted by a hair out of place, like a portrait hung crooked on the wall.

The best way to hide is to make them look at something else. This is the magician's secret.

Once, it was mine, too.

I didn't know what I was doing. All the nights I went out to the club dressed in what I called my "girl costume." I think the magician is supposed to be in on the trick. One night my friend and I stayed out until the bar closed and I was too drunk to drive myself home. Naturally, it fell to the guy pumping me full of whiskey to drive me back to his apartment. Outside, another guy shouted "good job dressing yourself tonight." I was wearing these brown over-the-knee boots I wore until they fell apart. They were my armor. A short, short minidress with long sleeves. What did he know? What did he know about dressing this body—and could he tell me?

I met Braden for the first time after graduating from high school. They were wearing skin-tight, hot pink skinny jeans and a lime green shirt, blonde hair gelled into an anime-protagonist swoop of spikes. "There's no way they'd be into me," we both thought, and went our separate ways.

Every intimate partner, a new dread. Finding the right moment for the disclaimer. My body a loud, emphatic answer to the wrong question. Wow, they seem so real! A big show, kissing the scars. I felt nothing. I made sounds like I was supposed to. Made it sound real.

I was a walking doll. Plastic, numb, stiff. Sex was just pain endured before closeness. One hookup stood me in front of a full-length mirror, exclaimed "look at you! You're super hot!" He'd left hickeys all over my neck and chest. He was studying to be a urologist. My navy-blue thong cut into my skin, the only article of clothing I was wearing. I closed my eyes.

After I graduated from the small liberal arts college in my hometown, I lost my mother for the first time. I wanted to move out, walk a different path from what she'd envisioned. I stayed holed up in my childhood bedroom for days, fearing confrontation, until I decided to get some space, stay at a friend's house for the night. After that, I never truly went home again.

Braden and I came out to each other as bisexual a couple months after we started dating. At the time, we looked like exactly one (weird) girl and one (weird) boy. Braden went first. "What a relief," I said— "because sometimes I'm a boy, and sometimes I'm a girl." A relief, that we would love each other either way. Any way.

Years later, when I told Braden's mother about my implants, she was surprised. She knew me so well by then, knew I was non-binary. But I'd kept the implants a secret from almost everyone, my whole life. Braden joked that they came across as "going the wrong direction." We laughed. The right direction was always: stay alive a little longer.

I fell in love with a star—not the thing itself, not the dense, swallowing mass, but the way its light looks from far away. From a human vantage point, the Horsehead Nebula is located just south of the easternmost star in Orion's belt. It is not referred to as a star-factory, but, rather, a *stellar nursery*.

My first apartment's windows sat on the ground. Someone could essentially fall in from the street. A basement apartment with four rooms: kitchen, stone bathroom with a dump-sink-turned shower, small living room, and tiny bedroom. There was only one door (the door to the bathroom) and one sink (the kitchen sink). I'd spent my last few days of that summer painting, the broken windows propped open with paint cans, breathing in fumes. Slowly, the living room turned to sage green and the bedroom a deep indigo-blue. I thought of my mother's HGTV obsession, how she pictured herself "flipping" rundown houses, turning them into something perfect, universally likeable.

My father tried to stay in touch, lurking on the margins of my life like a double agent. He kept it a secret from my mother. After I shaved half my head into an undercut—the asymmetry so affirming, so two-things-at-once—her vitriol exploded. "Your mom thinks you're...a lesbian," he said, his voice trembling with discomfort. I didn't answer. I said: "what do *you* think?" But we both didn't know. And I would never answer him.

There is essentially no sound in deep space—the large, seemingly empty areas between stars and planets. This is not a philosophical question, but one of vacuums and the way sound travels in molecular waves. The pain is about this kind of silence. A way to live from moment to moment by holding, desperately, to the nothingness in between.

I remember relief at the relatively low level of pain at my tattoo appointment—normally, when I expected my period to begin soon, tattoos felt like hell. I lasted for three hours during this appointment, the one and only time over the course of the sleeve that I saw a character through from outline to full color. It filled the inside of my right forearm, a looming figure of the old witch from *The Last Unicorn*, Mommy Fortuna. Her face was haggard, and she wore a brown slouch-y hat, color that needed to be touched up several times before it stuck.

The artist outlined one of Mommy Fortuna's gnarly hands in purple ink instead of black, and it swept upward around the side of my arm like she was casting a spell. The purple ink healed into an indigo blue. In the story, the unicorn meets Mommy Fortuna when she stumbles across a carnival the witch has orchestrated, casting illusion spells to turn ordinary creatures into myth. She keeps them all in tiny cages. The people come from miles around to see.

Mommy Fortuna's namesake, according to the author of the story, is the Roman goddess of fortune. She could bring good luck or bad, and was most often depicted wearing a blindfold. She personified life's unpredictability. The author added *Mommy.*

I had a vague idea that the emergency pregnancy tests might be under the bed, but I wasn't sure—and there was practically a universe of junk under there. The epicenter. My coworker, Mary, came straight home with me after our shift. She helped me lift the heavy mattress and box spring, so I could see everything at once. Almost immediately, my eyes landed on the small pink box: *First Response*.

Our sun is so dense it accounts for 99% of our solar system's mass, allowing it to dominate the other planets gravitationally. When I wrote about femininity in college, a professor told me in pop culture symbology, women were aligned with the moon because the moon does not give off its own light. Instead, the light we see from the moon is only a reflection of the sun's light.

Despite all the people in the world who had ever been pregnant, whether they wanted to be or not, I felt like the only one. The first person to walk on this planet. But this, too, was a fiction.

A con panna, I always reasoned, was the perfect drink because it was a straight shot to the heart from the espresso, and caloric content from the whipped cream. I started drinking more and more shots of espresso to stay upright through my barista shifts. It wasn't unusual for me to be tired. It wasn't out of the ordinary to take three-hour naps in the middle of the day. What did change was the way espresso affected me. It was as though, on the way to my mouth, it would disappear in thin air. The shots were very small, and made two at a time—both fitting in a tiny demitasse cup with a child-sized handle. They were golden-brown. If you do it right, they glow and beckon. A soft landing.

I convinced myself I could feel something moving in my stomach. I remember distinctly thinking I felt it in my stomach, and not my uterus, because my uterus was something of a fantasy I'd never bothered feeling. I didn't tell Braden at first. If I had, they might have been able to save me from the thought-loops I fell into.

The moon was formed some 30-50 million years after the Earth, countless years after the sun. This is just the start of the metaphor's undoing. They are rocks, and know nothing of light but what it does.

A few months before the positive pregnancy tests, I'd found a viral YouTube video. Someone who worked as an abortion counselor at Planned Parenthood discovered she was pregnant, and decided to film the procedure to dispel some myths. The tiny photo in the article on my Facebook news feed was immediately familiar.

I went to high school with Emma. We'd both been in a production of *Children of Eden*, a Steven Schwartz musical that our school chose because *Wicked* was hitting it so big. We went to a large public high school, by no means religiously-affiliated, but the show was loosely based on biblical stories—Adam and Eve, Cain and Abel, Noah and the Ark. Emma's voice was big, gutsy, improvisational. She played the lead.

I was given a packet of information, standard sheets of photocopied paper stapled together. In the state of Michigan in 2014, the law mandated you review this information for at least twenty-four hours before receiving an abortion. The law refers to it as "counseling." There are several pages detailing the procedures themselves, but the bulk of the pages are dedicated to information that is designed to deter people from getting an abortion. There are size markers for comparison: two nickels stacked together, a dime—many of them are money-related, so I can imagine holding it in my hand. The depictions, even with the references, are printed much larger than life.

Braden and I got donuts at our favorite place and ate them in Planned Parenthood's parking lot, talking with the windows rolled down. Ours was the first appointment of the day, but we still arrived early. We drank shitty coffee out of Styrofoam cups; the donuts could make any coffee taste good. Over the phone, a tech told me to wear comfortable clothes, heavy-duty pads, bring whatever we needed to occupy ourselves for up to four hours if need be. This, more than anything, gave me a sense of foreboding. She just wanted us to be prepared.

I walked to the counter slowly, wallet in hand. Thick, bullet-proof glass separated me from the receptionist. She smiled in a genuine way, not overly-friendly. She wasn't trying to comfort me. She didn't need to, because what she was doing was normal. Another normal day.

A trans-vaginal ultrasound. It felt exactly as invasive as it sounds. Legally required. In an amazing turn, it did not convince me that I was ready to give birth. No. It reminded me of my body—its soft stuff, set against cold plastic and metal. The technician printed a photo of the ultrasound—also required. She was gentle and solemn. She asked me if I wanted to see the photo. I did not. As she moved around the room with the printout in her hand, she was careful to keep it face-down, tilt it away from me.

The truth was I *had* imagined what was inside of me. I saw the cells more like a nebula—some huge and cosmic precursor—than a small-scale replica of a newborn baby. In my mind's eye, it was *something bigger* than what they'd wanted me to see.

Emma played Eve, and I played "The Snake." Meaning, the devil. There were six of us, in six-part harmony, who sang a syrupy jazz number with a gigantic snake-boa on our shoulders. Emma wore a white dress. She flitted among the six of us, singing a strange sort of duet, as we passed forbidden fruit among our twelve hands. When we spoke to her, we spoke simultaneously, in different registers. I danced as the tail end of the snake. Most notably, I extended an arm on the final beat of the song, and at the end of it, outstretched toward Emma, was a gigantic, real apple that barely fit in my palm.

I expected a crowd of protestors at the door, but there was just a middle-aged woman and an older man, sitting in folding chairs at the entrance to the parking lot, at the top of the hill. We arrived before they did, and only saw them on the way out. They seemed tired, disinterested—their sign "A CHILD, NOT A CHOICE" propped up lazily between them. Braden said "do you want to flip them off with me?" No. It's not that I felt empathy toward them, or that I was being the bigger person. I felt nothing toward them. I saw them exactly as they were.

When I was in high school, I bought the morning-after pill for a friend who was too young to legally buy it for herself. The pharmacist treated me with total disgust—maybe because he knew the pill was not for me, as she lurked through the aisles behind me, trying to look disinterested. I remembered this experience vividly as I studied the prescriptions written on Planned Parenthood RX pads. One prescription for an anti-nausea medication, and one for hydrocodone. I feared that the pharmacist would understand this combination and treat me that way again. I opted to fill the prescription for hydrocodone, and pocketed the sheet that called for the anti-nausea pill.

I figured I didn't need the anti-nausea pill because I'd never thrown up over the course of the pregnancy thus far. I was very wrong. Luckily, the secondary pills absorbed into my bloodstream—I held them against my gums—before the undoing started. Relieved when the blood came, but in so much pain. We kept referring to the "normal vs. not normal" pamphlet, unsure if we should pack up and go back to the clinic. Yes, this was normal. On the unfortunate end of the bell curve. Blood clots the size of lemons—all normal.

In the second act, toward the end, Mamma Noah passes away. She sings a song to all her children—the children of Eden. The entire cast was arranged around Emma, and the sole choreography was this—Emma, as Mamma Noah, connecting with each of us, individually, a shawl draped around her shoulders, as we mourned. I remember being choked up every time this scene rolled around, but especially so on closing night.

Like this brief day/ My light is nearly gone/ But through the night/ My children, you will go on./ You will know heartache/ Prayers that don't work/ And times of bitter circumstances./ But I still believe in second chances.

And there she is in the YouTube video, the same Emma. Her hair is dyed white-blonde, a change from the dark brunette she'd been in high school. She has the same eyes, the same wild intensity she had at that callback audition. In the video, she hums during the procedure. She smiles at the woman holding her hand. She says, over and over, how lucky she is. She remarks at how many hands there are to hold. "You deserve it," someone says. "Everyone deserves it," she says.

I'd heard that human beings are all made of stardust, that almost every element on Earth was formed at the heart of a star. I even pictured the embryo this way—the pinks and purples and white light of the nebulas I'd seen illustrated in books and on the Internet, surrounded by utter darkness. Created by an unexpected breaking-open.

I thought of the way we make wishes. The way fate is supposed to be written in the stars. The way we map them and try to understand. Light a candle once a year, remember this nebula forming inside me. A galaxy of potential that didn't need to become anything more in order to be something that mattered—something that had a kind of life. I thought of the way the light from stars we see in the sky may be reaching us long, long after the star is gone.

The Horsehead Nebula is a dark nebula, which means it is a type of interstellar cloud so dense it obscures the light from anything behind it. Large dark nebulae are visible to the discerning naked eye, appearing as patches of darkness even blacker than the night sky.

When we moved out of the basement apartment, packed up everything we owned (not much) for Pittsburgh, the walls were rife with black mold. We'd found a new place with sunlight and two sinks, a new city. Even so, we cried. Took photos of what little light managed to roll through the barred window.

A year afterward, I met up with a friend who confided in me when we were in college, when she needed support during her abortion. We'd been apart for years, but when I intimated that there was something I wanted to tell her, she knew it before I spoke. Such relief, our knowing together. Embarking on the long walk back to my car from the restaurant, we discovered the life-sized skeleton of a unicorn drawn in sidewalk chalk in front of a tattoo parlor. Soon after, the sky opened up into torrential rain.

The light that reaches us after the star's supernova *is* the star, just as much as it is not the star. It's the memory of the star, and all that's left of the star's present moment. Born of a patch of night sky somehow darker than the night sky. The way light experiences a year. Whatever I am. And still moving forward.

In graduate school, a museum curator visited our poetry workshop and asked us all to draw five stars, however we chose, on a blank piece of paper. I drew five five-pointed stars, the way I learned when I was small, sprawling across the page. She pointed out that we all drew the stars in similar ways— the five-pointed star, Star of David, asterisk. Little else. That these kinds of images—even as complex as a star—can be carved down into well-worn patterns in our minds. Because we see them so often in these forms, we don't imagine far past emoji. "Ouch," my friend said, "that hurts."

My father said more about me in his toast at our wedding than he'd said in roughly two decades of my life. He said I "always made the right choice." A political statement, a friend called it. I wore a sleeveless dress—just the sleeve of tattoos. I thought of him a year or two earlier, approaching me like he was going in for a hug, begging me not to get the sleeve. "For me," he said. "Just...don't do it, for me?"

Shortly after we moved back to Michigan, freshly burned out from graduate school and more depressed than I'd been in a long time, I dreamed of the body beneath my bed. Often, I dreamed my parents had murdered someone and I was helping them dispose of the body. This was different, though. The corpse did not look like me, but I knew she was me. My corpse, even though I was sleeping above her on the bed. I didn't know about her until the swarm of black flies climbed itself into hills, bubbling up between the mattress and the headboard. I covered her face with a sheet. Not my face, but my face. Turned to leather with neglect. How would I identify the cadaver if the body was mine?

Our first June back, we dug a grave and buried the vegetable garden. Braden and I suited up in masks and goggles, so as not to breathe in the trillions of spores breaking into the air as we shoveled it all into the wheelbarrow. A couple months before, on our anniversary, I'd declared our third year married "the year of growth." Braden built the raised beds as a gift, three big rectangles of untreated cedar. We filled them with store-bought dirt and plants, thinking we were playing it safe buying everything the first time around. The plants spent their first days in torrential downpours like we'd never seen. The soil sat bloated with rainwater even when the sky turned to blazing sun and temperatures over one hundred degrees. You would think we'd *meant* to cultivate blight.

It sprang up over the tomatoes and zucchini first, and I tried to pick it away with my bare hands. I thought I could clear it out, cleanse the garden of contamination. I wish I could tell you I only peeled it away once, and it never returned. As it worsened, I searched the Internet for just one source that didn't insist the whole garden be destroyed at once. We were just at the beginning. I'd already eaten a strawberry from a plant half-consumed by fungus. It was so small and sweet. The first of many, I thought. Braden dug a hole large enough to cover all the dirt at least a foot below the surface. The sun still hadn't let up. When I upended the wheelbarrow into the pit, the weight of it almost pulled me in, too.

The moon is not a lesser version of the sun, but we can't live there either way. So I don't care. Maybe what I think doesn't matter. Just—whether our god is in the sky or of the earth. Whether I'm a person or a pot of soil. A vessel for something else. It matters that the planets move constantly, even if horoscopes aren't real. Instead of imagining ways to save this world, we dream up futures where we find another planet, leave this one behind. Capitalism doesn't solve problems, it just destroys. It can't create a planet. Just billionaires, and toys.

We reached our depths in the winter of 2020-2021. Once, the sun shined through the window and we dropped what we were doing to bundle up and head outside to catch some. We found a tree not too far into the woods, struck by lightning seemingly moments before. It was charred and dying, taking its time. Big red globs of sap wept through the cracks, a brilliant final effort to heal. For a moment, with the sun radiating through it, I thought it still glowed with fire.

Plants go into dormancy to rest. Like a soft-launch death. That's what I did. I had that feeling again, like I was watching my life from behind a screen. Every single thing was Something I Didn't Prepare For. My therapist told me to nail the escape routes shut. But I only had hammers, no nails.

An oncologist begins to understand metastasis by studying
the invasive species of mussels taking over the Great Lakes.
Or, not so much studying, but allowing himself to be changed
by metaphor. He chooses seed and soil to describe how a
tumor takes root in the body. Why would we study the seed
and forget the environment that makes it possible? A kind of
growth I'm not in on yet. But I will be. The mussels in the
Great Lakes, eating all the phytoplankton until the water is
clear all the way down, so clear you can see the shipwrecks
from the surface.

I am the soil and cancer is the seed. I carry it inside of me. So many little seeds with sails attached like dandelions floating along, no way to tell where they will stick. Not a whether, but a when. What kind of soil am I? Am I letting it flourish? Is that my fault now, too?

Plucking wolves from one island ecosystem and dropping them into another. The science writer wonders: "Perhaps we are always, forever, just studying ourselves…" Watch as two wolves who could revitalize the gene pool turn and walk away for seemingly no reason. Maybe we will never know. But the things we could've known by now, if we knew how to look.

We were dying. We weren't going to make it through the winter. We took every chance we could to stave it off, slipping up over us like a heavy blanket, snuffing us out.

I dream of big haunted houses. I'm the one haunting them. I've lived there as a ghost for years, long enough to know every crack and crevice. Still, I find secret wings long-abandoned. Houses so big, no one could live in the whole thing. I think—oh! I can just live here. There's plenty of room. A whole place no one knows about. They won't even know I'm here.

Something like a conversation began to fester in my mother's mouth. The right conversation to talk me out of it, talk me out of my life. Braden was making me ill, she thought, keeping me from her. She would tell anyone she could, maybe it helped with the pain of carrying it. The pain of not being able to change the world, change someone else, with words.

My mother sent Braden a text hoping to stage an "intervention." She thought they would keep this a secret from me. I was letting my body become something else, and I needed to be stopped. I needed to be helped, shaken by the shoulders maybe. *They know their own body and how to care for it,* Braden replied. Maybe that was it—the point of no return.

I just wanted to be free. Even if only in my mind. Even if my body never caught up. I was dying and I wanted to live. What were we even doing all day, in that too-big house they helped us buy, so close to theirs? She would drive by over and over again, looking to see if my car was in the driveway, texting me *are you home? Are you home?*

Summer was turning to fall on an ordinary day in 2019. I was listening to a podcast, just getting out of the shower. I dried my blunt bob with a towel. I stared out the bathroom window to the sunflowers towering in the raised beds outside. And I realized I'm nonbinary.

After everything, I was letting a word hold me back. There wasn't a pronoun that fit me, and they/them didn't feel like it fit either. But why not use it? Why not try? I thought—I'm a poet, I should know better than anyone that most words don't exactly fit. I stopped worrying about how they fit, caring more about how they felt. There was no going back after that.

I didn't expect the chickens to feel so much like *birds*. I'd grown up with parrots, hand-feeding at a local pet shop just to be close to them. Of course, chickens are birds just as much as they are holdovers from prehistoric times. This is never clearer than when they are babies, especially in their in-between phases, when the fluff is gone and they look like little raptors who forgot to get dressed in the morning.

I drove, admittedly, too far to retrieve four sentient fluff balls from a hobby farmer named Amanda. Her farm's Google listing brought me to the front door of her house. I was nervous—looking more and more queer as the pandemic stretched on. It was already spring, 2021. I passed through acres of middle Michigan, dotted with signs for Trump, signs threatening hellfire, countless billboards for weed dispensaries. When Amanda emerged, carrying a little box with holes punched around the sides, I immediately relaxed. She wore sparkly pink and blue eyeshadow, vivid blush, a dress over pajama bottoms. She handed me the little box of chicks, impossibly lightweight but moving and peeping vigorously. We could have talked about them for hours.

There are several ways to sex baby chicks ranging from inaccurate to inhumane. All of it is more or less a guess. I opted to gently stretch a tiny wing to see if all the feathers were about the same length (potential rooster) or if they had a little section of slightly longer ones (potential hen). We weren't planning on a rooster, but we knew the odds of an accidental one were high. I declared Donna our "rooster candidate," but we wouldn't know for sure until she was older and her true feathers started coming in, or until she attempted to lift her voice in the trademark rooster crow.

They say to expect a twenty percent loss when calculating how many chicks to buy. This is part of a larger, more complex set of rules for raising fowl jokingly referred to as "chicken math." Stubbornly, we wanted four chickens and bought four chicks. It would be different for us, we thought. Two named Leslie and Anne, both Barnevelders, a heritage breed Amanda hoped to help conserve. Two more named Donna and April, olive-egger types of Amanda's own design. They say not to name them until they're older—meant to help you get less attached. Remember, the twenty percent inevitability. I thought we'd get lucky. We would care more. And I would've named her anyway. It wouldn't have hurt any less.

After Anne-the-chick died, we brought home two ducklings from an old friend's farm. Not as replacement, so much as distraction from the heartache. Bonnie and Marcie grew much faster than the chickens. We fed them a niacin supplement to make sure their legs would support their rapid weight-gain. Marcie was a Cayuga, nearly double the size of Bonnie (Khaki Campbell) fully-grown. The chickens remained awkward, naked dinosaurs for weeks after Marcie came into her own as the flock leader. We laughed every time she put Donna, then an adolescent rooster, in their place. Her size came with a commanding presence.

Bonnie and Marcie were in love. In the water, Bonnie would climb atop Marcie and mate with her—their roles unexpectedly reversed. "Are birds usually this queer, or did we make them like this?" We joked. Now I can say the answer is yes—they are that queer. Marcie was the boss, and she was a bossy bottom.

We came to understand the unspoken language of the birds. We looked up to the sky, scanning for predators. Sometimes the specter of an airplane would set off the alarms. They were right to be on alert. We lived at the edge of a bog, a vivid ecosystem, danger at every turn. A constant dance between freedom and safety. In the end, we would open the coop door in the morning, and everyone did their best to return at dusk. Another version of myself worried about the birds so much, wanted so badly to keep them all safe, that they never would've left the coop at all.

I came home from the grocery store to an eerie silence in the backyard. April and Leslie were huddled together beneath the lilac bush, impossibly still. The sense of wrongness deepened. At the other end of the yard, Donna stood protectively with Bonnie. That was when I knew Marcie was gone. I didn't have time to fear I would never find her—our younger dog, Mavis, barely older than a puppy, solemnly led me straight to the body, like she knew, she was waiting to guide me. Marcie's throat was cut, chest cavity swarmed with feasting bees. Black feathers scattered and clumped across the forest floor. None of these details explained what happened, but I knew: when the threat approached, Marcie stepped forward. She got in the way. She stood between the predator and her family, gave them time to get to safety.

I found a box in the garage and lifted her body into it, disrupting the decomposition process so swiftly taking root. I sobbed until my chest hurt, a stinging swarm. Braden rushed home from work. I could barely look at them. I couldn't explain. This part of me had fought and died. I dug a hole beneath the lilac bush as I wept. Jumping onto the shovel with all my weight to cut into the hard summer earth. A couple times I missed, almost falling, screaming with grief. Braden emerged from the house, gently took the shovel from my hands. That night, Bonnie called and called into the darkness, letting herself hope a blue-black figure might emerge from the night, come home to her, settle her weight in the coop's doorway, keep watch.

Bonnie and Donna became inseparable, like Donna felt an imperative to protect her in memory of Marcie. Donna and Bonnie fell in love, we called them "mom and dad." They roamed the world together, April and Leslie never far. Once, my dad stood at our front door, car still running as they waddled past. "Are they...choosing that?" he asked. Braden and I exchanged a complicated look. Yes, a love you don't understand can be the most natural thing in the world. A choice so obvious there's no need to explain.

We used all pronouns to refer to Donna. She/her came naturally—for months, we didn't know. When we did, the occasional he/him, though it never felt quite right. They/them for all the moments in between, the inadequacy of words—something Donna would never feel the need to contemplate.

We witnessed Donna kick a hawk out of the air more than once, a marvel of agility and precision almost comical compared to their resting state of bumbling worry. Once, Donna buried a sharp spur in the belly of a swooping hawk, an imprint of the hunter's full wingspan marking the snow. "Stop—" my parents interrupted urgently, as we were telling the story "—it's a *boy*, right? The rooster is a *he?!*"

Six duck eggs sat in the controlled heat and humidity of a plastic incubator in our living room the day we found out the Supreme Court struck down *Roe V. Wade*. Bonnie sat on a nest of her own unfertilized eggs in the coop, going broody just as we planned for her ducklings to arrive. Only one emerged. I watched her hatch. She thought I was her mother.

I candled the eggs at each stage of development, waiting impatiently for a week to pass, then two, then four. I took each egg into a dark bathroom, held them in the glow of my iPhone's flashlight. Two were empty from the beginning, their insides one diffuse, formless cloud. I was shocked when the other four developed embryos, if only because a pessimistic voice in my head told me nothing would grow in the dark.

It was bad bird math to incubate only six eggs, let alone casually-collected ones from a friend who wasn't really trying for more ducks. I kept fastidious notes on each embryo—at first, just little specs in the light, then a spider web of veins stretching out into the shell's space. One embryo moved incessantly, wiggling in place like it was jumping to the beat of unheard music. Sometimes I would sing to them at the top of my soprano range, because Bonnie and Marcie loved that when they were little. Days before the hatch, I swore I saw two eggs wobbling, stirring. But only the one hatched. One perfect duckling, who, from the very first moment, seemed too big ever to have fit inside a shell at all.

I could've left it there. One perfect duckling, focusing its tiny lazer beam of love on us. Still, I needed to look closer. I needed to crack open the remaining eggs—the ones that promised they were growing all along. I knocked a metal spoon against the first shell, wincing. Every instinct told me not to do it. Thick fluid and blood around the curled, dark body of a duckling-that-almost-was.

The problem was apparent immediately: shrink-wrapping. Insufficient humidity causes the protective membrane inside the shell to dry out, creating a prison instead. My breath hitched as I knocked against the last egg, the one I'd seen moving only days before. Its body bulged just beneath the sloped walls of the place that kept it safe until it didn't. Maybe I could have saved this duckling, if I'd known enough to add more water to the incubator, even mist the eggs with a spray bottle. Maybe, if I'd been brave enough to crack the egg open and pull it out myself. None of that happened. But at least now, I know.

Roe V. Wade disappeared overnight. Many Americans never imagined it possible. But I knew. It echoed through my body. I felt a renewed urgency to get the implants out. Because there is no limit to what they will take in the name of consequences.

I knew what I needed long before I knew the words for it: top surgery. If I'd kept performing cis-ness, maybe it all would've happened without question. Maybe I would write this from a comfortable place, no soreness and strain from displaced muscles, compounding scar tissue. I'll admit, I thought I could word the text in a way that would make her see it. *It's time to talk about removing my implants. I think I want to go the double mastectomy route, like you did.*

If this is about your new gender identity, I want no part of that.

My father dropped a letter off at our house. A blank envelope. He was pulling out of the driveway as I opened the door. Maybe that will be the last time I ever see him. Should I tell you all the details of the letter? No. No—for everything I've made of words, everything I will make—theirs were unremarkable. I will give them this: *one day you will look back on this and thank us.*

They were right about that.

I'd planted the vegetable starts in their permanent homes in the ground and the raised beds. Countless flower seedlings were emerging from the soil around a wicker bench, where we imagined ourselves sitting to admire the vegetables. We'd reinforced the bottom of the fence with smaller wire mesh to ward off the rabbits from the year before. I also planned a "decoy garden," near the edge of the woods beneath the lilac bush, an extra patch of herbs and greens for the wildlife to peruse at their pleasure. But I never got the chance to plant it.

Sometimes I would get home and the deadbolt would be locked, even though I never left it that way. Braden experienced it, too. This made no sense—until suddenly, it did. Not a ghost's hand turning the lock after us, but my mother's hand locking away a secret. Without us knowing. Little moments when we were both out of the house. A spark of fear connected a circuit. The night of the letter, we barricaded ourselves inside. We planned our escape.

I love you, my father texted. *I love you, you are going down the wrong path.*

Who knows how many more times he would've sent it, if they hadn't taken my phone. If he knew my new number.

Do they remember the fifteen-year expiration date? I never imagined they could forget. Braden talked to my dad over the phone several times before we left the state, shouldering the burden of contact. They reminded my dad about my mother's double mastectomy, preventative—like mine could be. "Well you don't know the whole story," he responded. "She did have breast cancer."

She did have breast cancer. All these years, my doctors working from an incomplete medical history. Blank cells and unchecked boxes. Risk, jumping into my throat like a fist.

"So we're just supposed to wait until they have cancer?" I couldn't see Braden, but I knew them well enough to know they were phone-pacing furiously in their childhood backyard. My mother-in-law stood at the kitchen window, catching moments of the conversation, proud of her kid. "Yes," my dad replied. Yes, wait until the cancer has already arrived, already taken shape.

"Your child will never speak to you again, you know that? All because we're not broken up enough about some fucking breast tissue."

My dad cried. He's only cried a handful of times over the course of my life. Braden hung up, came back inside. Continued saving our lives.

"Is there anything you want to do to commemorate our last night here?" Braden stood outside the shower as I bathed. I didn't want to be separated for even a moment. No, I just wanted to keep going together. We'd already lived every night like it was our last.

Our time was running out. We had to leave Michigan. The rest of the flock was in a box, waiting to drive up north to their new farm. But we couldn't catch Donna. I left them, feeling gutted they were being separated from us, from their family. We spent hours trying to catch them, until we couldn't anymore. Until it wasn't even safe for us to be there. I can't forgive myself for leaving them—even if I knew she would find them and save them. Or, at least, call the right person to do it for her.

I brought you into this world. I can take you out.

I'm in the house I grew up in, a winding, strange, 90's-rich-people design. It's laid out just like I remember it—a place that exists only in my mind now. My brother isn't there—he's older than me, maybe sleeping at a friend's place. My room is past his, a turn off the hallway near the bathroom. Something is there. In my room. Someone. I don't quite catch a glimpse—a shoulder slipping through the door frame. It's just me here. Just me and my mom sleeping alone in the big bedroom. She and my dad are fighting and he went somewhere else. I go to her, but she tells me to leave. I'm annoying. I have to go back to the room, I have no choice. There is only her room or mine. I see the specter lurking, flitting behind the gap of the open doorway. Somehow, there's room to build a full run down the hallway. I scream. I scream. I'm going to confront it.

Braden wakes me up in our bed in Pittsburgh. It's 2023. I remember everything. "It's okay," they say. Olive stands over me like a sentinel. Mavis climbs under the covers and presses her whole body against mine.

"I just need to get really swole. Like, work out so much that these make sense as pecs," I joked, flexing. "Make sense?" was all Braden managed, with a smile. We were laughing. We kept laughing. We looked out the front window of our new apartment, the porch garden promising tomatoes and herbs and eggplants, one day soon.

Rich people often mistake investment for love. But money is not a language. Power is not meaning.

My body is not a problem to be solved. My body is an experience, one only I am having. My body is living. Dying, too. Another binary blurred. I called to make an appointment for a consultation with a surgeon with an extensive background in top surgery. The person who took my information was gentle, anticipating sore spots. My heart dropped when she warned me this doctor was not authorized to perform a mastectomy, as that requires further specialization and skill. She heard the fear in my voice. "You know," she added, "top surgery alone will reduce your risk." At first, I didn't understand. "Top surgery will reduce your risk because you will have less breast tissue." As simple as that. I couldn't solve everything at once. I couldn't control the future—but I could choose what was best for now.

The woman on the phone asked "...and when did you know you needed the implants removed?" One of the screening questions meant to measure my certainty. "The moment I got them," I replied, not trying to be dramatic. Still, she gasped. She said "oh, dear." It felt very human. My pain, her compassion. I always knew they would need to come out. After them, just the boyish chest I had before. But I had practice telling the story. I'm grateful for that. I had practice, thanks to you.

It took my body a long time to wake from its winter. The roots grew, stretched, changed, but the surface remained the same. For some people, the seasons shift all on their own, the cycles repeat themselves the same way every time. They don't worry about waiting. They don't wonder what the sun's life is like.

The sun, too, is a star. A star that made all of this. You and me, the same.

I wish I could know my queer ancestors. The ones who lived so I could live.

For now, I'm here. Trying to live so you can live. And I feel it. I feel your love here, too.

notes

pg. 5: Facts about outer space included in this book reflect industry knowledge at the time of writing. Most information was gleaned from NASA's website, nasa.gov.

pg. 15: I have come to understand myself as intersex in the context of my experience with PCOS. This is not to say that every person with this syndrome feels the same way. PCOS can manifest in many different forms, and does not always impact sex and gender markers like it has in my case. This is also not to say that women with PCOS who seek treatment for these symptoms are any less the women they say they are. It must be noted, however, that medication like spironolactone is *absolutely* gender-affirming care—for cis- and trans- people alike.

pg. 19: This quote is from Elaine Scarry's book *The Body in Pain: The Making and Unmaking of the World*, Oxford University Press, 1987.

pg. 43: All of my tattoos are the work of artist Nicholas Rivera of Daybreak Tattoo in southwest Michigan.

pg. 52: Sections pertaining to abortion law in this book reflect Michigan law at the time of writing in 2014. The law is different from state to state, and has already changed in many ways. I encourage everyone to familiarize themselves with the current language of their state's law, and to interrogate stipulations like this deceitful "counseling" packet.

pg. 60: Abortion via pill takes place in two phases: first, the mifepristone pill stops the pregnancy from progressing. I was administered this pill by a doctor at Planned Parenthood. I was sent home to take the second medicine, misoprostol, which causes the uterus to shed its tissue. The phrase "blood clots the size of lemons" is language taken from pamphlets I received from Planned Parenthood.

pg. 61: Lyrics from the title song of the musical *Children of Eden* by Stephen Schwartz.

pg. 69: This is a scene from Yona Harvey's graduate poetry workshop at The University of Pittsburgh.

pg. 77: This section refers to Siddhartha Mukherjee's essay "Cancer's Invasion Equation," originally published in *The New Yorker*, included in the anthology *The Best American Science and Nature Writing 2018* edited by Sam Kean and published by Houghton Mifflin Harcourt.

pg. 79: This page refers to another essay from *The Best American Science and Nature Writing 2018*: "The Island Wolves" by Kim Todd, originally published in *Orion*.

pg. 85: This page refers to the podcast Food 4 Thot, specifically their episode "Bye Bye, Binary!" with guest Alok Menon, first released on March 17th, 2019. I have followed Alok's career closely since they were a tumblr poet, and the podcast from its inception. This episode gave me permission to be myself in two ways: by complicating my understanding of pronouns, and emphasizing that "coming out" is not a compulsory gateway to queerness.

pg. 90: The "they" of "they say," in this case, is the subreddit r/backyardchickens.

pg. 116: "I brought you into this world. I can take you out" ...is a phrase my mother said to me often throughout my life, in modulating tones. I attempted to find the source of this quote for the sake of this book, but it is so ubiquitous in so many variations, it was difficult to find its roots.

acknowledgments

My unending gratitude to Alex Alberto and Caroline Shannon, without whom this book would not exist. The two of you gave me the opportunity to make my first book exactly what I wanted it to be—something that feels particularly important given its subject matter.

I'm truly honored to have worked with Rachel Ake and Alison Cnockaert, our cover designer and interior designer, respectively. Every element of this book is beyond anything I could have imagined. Thank you for seeing my work in a way only you two could.

To everyone who contributed to the Kickstarter campaign—all of this would not have been possible without every single one of you. Your support quite literally made it happen! A special shoutout to our founding backer Robyn Lyn. Here's to more queer books in the future.

I would not be the writer I am today without the teachers and colleagues I met at The University of Pittsburgh. Yona Harvey and Dawn Lundy-Martin truly saw me, even before I fully saw myself. Angie Cruz is the reason why I finished the MFA even when I felt I didn't belong. Peter Trachtenberg encouraged an early draft of this book.

To all of my writerly siblings from Pitt: Kelly Andrews, Cameron Barnett, Ariana Brown, Stephanie Cawley, Kazumi Chin, S. Brook Corfman, Malcolm Friend, Emily Hopkins, Morgan Kayser, Jessica Lanay, Michelle Lin, Lucia LoTempio, Nina Sabak, Suzannah Spaar, Gabrielle Ralambo-Rajerison, Caleb Washburn, and Anna Weber...what a privilege to learn with you and from you back then, and to continue to do so now.

I'm not sure where we would be without the Gofundme Krystal Gast created when she learned of the events described at the end of this book. Every single person who donated played a role in granting us safe passage to a new life. You demonstrated the power of community, and I will never forget it.

To every beloved person who was a part of Rose Gold Coffee Company, both in front of and behind the counter—it was all worth it because of you.

A special thank you to the Fairchild family and to Commonplace Coffee for giving us a place to land in Pittsburgh—especially Soren, who opened their home to us and welcomed us at our worst. To Frank and Belle Battista, who extended a standing invitation to aid in our return, even before we realized our situation was untenable. We had strength in our worst moments because of you. And to Viggo and Zali, who teach us every day what is possible for the future.

To all the people who have helped me rebuild my heart and find my strength: Pam Poley, Ariana Fay Calvin Laine, Toi Derricotte, and Zee Winters Anweiler, to name a few.

To the Strayer family—Chris, Greg, and Madi—I'm so proud to know you, to be known by you, and to share the most badass last name possible.

To Braden—I love doing this life with you. I can hardly believe my luck. Let's do it again in a million more lifetimes.

And, finally, to Olive—the dog who was a part of my soul, who kept me on this planet when I felt there was nothing else left. I know you waited until I was safe before you moved on from this plane. At last, I'm at a loss for words. I will spend the rest of my life living up to the way you loved me.

content warnings

Abortion: 50, 52, 53, 54, 55, 56, 58, 59, 60, 62, 67

Animal Death: 90, 91, 94, 95, 102, 103

Cancer: 16, 17, 18, 77, 78, 112, 113, 121

Depression/Mental Health: 7, 28, 71, 75, 76, 80

Disordered Eating and Fatphobia: 3, 4, 7, 13

Familial Abuse: 83, 84, 109, 110, 112, 113, 116

Familial Estrangement: 35, 40, 107, 110, 111, 112, 113, 115, 116

Homophobia: 40, 110

Medical Trauma: 7, 12, 25, 27, 52, 55, 59, 112, 113, 122

Pregnancy Loss: 6

Sexual Assault: 31, 33, 34, 55

Suicidality: 7, 28, 76, 80

Transphobia: 98, 106, 107, 110, 113

K.G. Strayer is a trans/non-binary writer and artist from Kalamazoo, Michigan, and Pittsburgh, Pennsylvania. They live and write across genre. *Stellar Nursery: On My (Trans) Body and My Choice* is their first book. Follow along on Instagram @kgstrayer, or visit kgstrayer.com for more.

www.ingramcontent.com/pod-product-compliance
Lightning Source LLC
Chambersburg PA
CBHW020400130626
46549CB00006B/2360